IN MY TREE

DUAA JAMAL KARIM

ISBN: 978-0-244-55957-1

Dedication

For my father
who taught me that
to define
is to limit.

For my mother
who is my light in the darkness
my moon, my hero, my home.

This World Betrays
Imam Ali

ABOUT

Ali Ibn Abi Talib AS was the Commander of the Faithful. The Lion. The Knight. The Saint.

There are many great poets and writers in history, but none so great as the Imam, whose words ring true to any day and age. This is a narrated, contemporary version of the beautiful narrations in modern day English. Though every effort has been made to present an accurate translation of the sayings, the author takes full responsibility for any mistakes and errors perceived in the translation and seeks forgiveness from the Almighty for the same.

Often, we forget that this life is just a test and a burden on those who strive to attain the glory of this world. It clearly isn't a coincidence that throughout the time of man, the focal point in all the narrations and teachings is learning how to accept being alone, and that silence is key. That this is it. When you are alone, your mind is clearer and it actually gives you focus and a calmness that cannot be put into words, but only felt.

It is not about being lonely, but what we fail to realise is that our soul demands to be felt. Pain demands to be felt. We owe it to our soul to be in one with it and to listen to its silence. To understand it because surely if we cannot understand our own self, then how do we expect anyone else to? Even worse, we are in fact creating our own storm by this false expectation and then jumping right into the tornado of emotions, thereby invoking a vicious cycle that ensures heartache. We feel betrayed when people do not understand us, yet we do not understand ourselves.

This is the root of all our problems and in the words of the Great Imam Ali, "The greatest knowledge is to know yourself."

Such is the condition of life
One day
It favour's you and makes you laugh
One day
It betrays you and makes you weep

Nothing hurts a good soul
And a kind heart
More
Than to live amongst people
who cannot understand it

This entire world
Is not worth
A single tear

Nobody can guard your secret
Better than you
So do not blame anyone for revealing
Your secret
For you could not hide them yourself.
Your secret
Is your prisoner
Which if let loose will make you
It's prisoner.

Do not take someone's silence
As his pride
Perhaps,
He is busy
Fighting
With his self

We have those who will
Love us
Even if we cut them in to pieces

We have those who will
Hate us
Even if we feed them pure honey

I will be
Patient
Until even
Patience
Tires of my
Patience

Often,
It is you
Who do yourself
The most harm

Be sure
That there is something
Waiting for you
After much patience
To astonish you
To a degree
That you forget
The bitterness
Of the pain

The truth
That hurts
Is better
Than the lie
That brings joy

The deception of hope
Wastes time
And brings
Death closer

Perhaps
You are the cause of your own
Misfortune

People do not
Hurt us
Our hopes from them
Hurt us

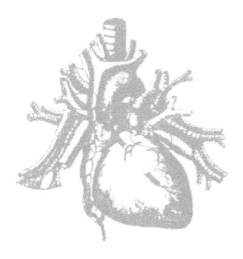

I have never
Blamed anyone
For divulging my secret
When I was more
unaccommodating of it
Than them

Remain silent
Until you are requested to speak
For that is better than speaking
Until you are requested to
Become silent

Do not run
After the one
who tries to
Avoid you

He who knows humanity
Seeks solitude

Ask
In order to understand and do not
Ask
In order to find fault

Forgive what they do not know

Every word you speak
Is recorded
Every deed you do
Is witnessed
So speak good
And do good

Do not betray anyone
Who places his trust in you
Even if he
Betrays you

Do not reveal his secrets
Even if he
Reveals yours

Your secret
Is safe with no one
But yourself

This world
With its delusions
My soul
With its offences, and
My delays
Have deceived me

Your sickness is from you
But you do not perceive it
Your remedy is within you
But you do not sense it
You presume you are a small entity
But within you is enfolded
The entire universe
You are indeed the evident book
By whose alphabets the hidden
Becomes manifest

Therefore
You have no need to look
Beyond yourself
What you seek is within you
If only you reflect

No sadness lasts forever
No happiness lasts forever

Among men
Only two are fortunate;
The one with a loyal friend, and
The one whose mother prays for him

Days are surely three
One passed
And you do not hope for it
One is present
And you will unavoidably meet it
One is the day to come
And you cannot trust it

Words pierce
Deeper
Than swords

The best deed of a great man is
To forgive
And forget

Death
Could not be held back

Life
Could not be prolonged

One
Who adopts patience
Will never be deprived of success

Though
It may take a long time to reach him

Being sincere
Is the best
Of actions

He who trusts
The world
The world
Betrays him

Take only what you need
The rest is only a burden

The greatest knowledge
Is to know yourself

In solitude
I found my sanctuary

The more you know
The less you speak

Do not hate what
You do not know
For the greater part of knowledge
Consists of what
You do not know

Do not develop friendship
With the enemy of your friend
Otherwise your friend
Will turn into an enemy

Books
Are the gardens of scholars

Nobility is a matter of good intellect
And good conduct
Not of lineage and descent

There is enough
Light
For one who wants to
See

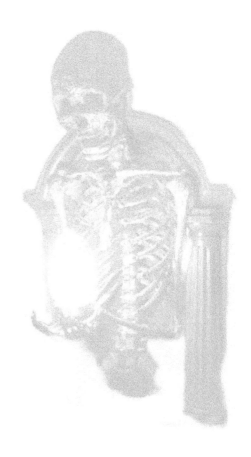

Anger
It begins with madness
And
Ends with regret

Death is near, and
Our mutual company is short

Who speaks to you
About others
Will speak about you
To others

A liar's biggest punishment
In this world
Is that even his truth is rejected
In this world

A little which lasts
Is better than
Much which brings
Grief

Authority
Power, and
Wealth
Do not change a man
They only reveal him

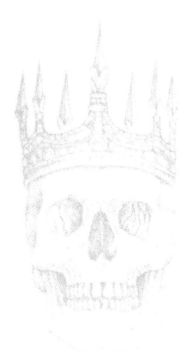

The ignorant man
Does not understand the learned
For he has never been learned himself

But

The learned man
Understands the ignorant
For he was once ignorant himself

Not every man
With a heart is understanding
Not every man
With ears is a listener
Not every man
With eyes is able to see

The words of God
Are the best medicine of the heart

People
Are like waves of the ocean
Some
Cover you with the tides of refreshment
Others
Drown you in floods of turmoil

Be cautious of
Lies big and small
Seriously and in jest
For if a man
Tells a small lie
He will have
The audacity
To tell a big lie

When words come from the heart
Of anyone
They find a place in the heart
Of another

Honesty saves you
Even if you fear it

Detachment
Is not that you should own nothing
But
That nothing should own you

The disease of the
Heart
Is worse than
The disease of the
Body

The world cannot
Defeat you
Until you accept the
Defeat

Wait patiently
And everything
Shall reveal itself
To you

Forgive
Those who have
Wronged you

Silence
Is the garden of
Thought

Understanding
Is what makes
Relationships

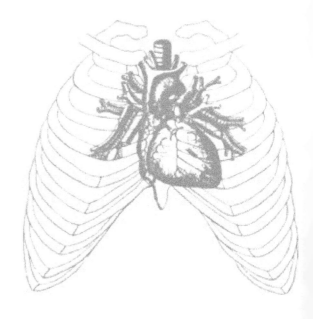

Honesty

Is divine language

Anxiety

Magnifies the calamity

Jealousy

Is the worst disease

Sorrow

Makes a man old before his time

Conquer

Thyself

Nothing

Hurts the heart more than sins

Accept

The apology even if it's not sincere

Leave

What leaves you

Know

Then speak

Leave

Alone what does not concern you

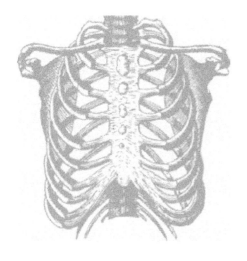

Knowledge

Gives life to the soul

Modesty

Prevents one from ugly actions

Achieve

Your goals in silence

Oftentimes
It is anger that reveals
True feelings of
People

Surely silence
Can be the most
Eloquent reply

The most
Ignorant
Of those who are
Ignorant
Is the one who trips over
The same stone
Twice

Good intentions
Are the most
Beautiful of secrets

Live amongst people in such a manner
That if you die
They weep over you
And if you live
They crave your company

You are part of me
Nay,
You are all of me
What hurts you hurts me
What kills you kills me

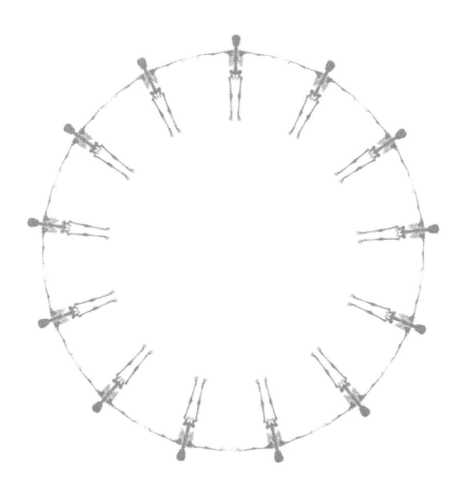

Yesterday
Is gone forever
Tomorrow
Is uncertain

Do for this life as if you are going to live
Forever
Do for the afterlife as if you are going to die
Tomorrow

Life is but the shadow of a cloud
The dream of a sleeper

How foolish is man
Ruins the present worrying
Of the future
Yet weeps in the future
Recalling the past

You presume you are a small entity
But within you is enfolded the entire
Universe

Do not tell your Lord
You have a great problem
Tell your problems
You have a great Lord

Do not wait
For tomorrow
For tomorrow
May never come

Give your enemy a thousand chances
To become your friend but,
Do not give your friend
A single chance to become
Your enemy

A fool repeats
The same mistake twice
Without learning

Let go of your
Pride
Put down your
Arrogance
Remember your
Grave

People often hate those things
Which they do not know
Or cannot understand

Richest
Of all the
Riches is
Knowledge

Knowledge
Is better than wealth
Knowledge
Protects you while
You have to protect
Your wealth

Know
That God is more kind to you
Than
You are to yourself

Your greatest enemy is
Yourself

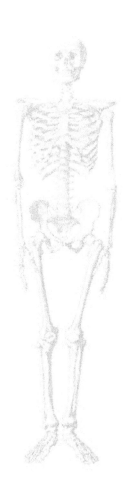

Give
And do not remember
Receive
And do not forget

Every hopeful person
Continues seeking
Every fearful person
Runs away

When good befalls you
Be thankful
When harm befalls you
Be patient

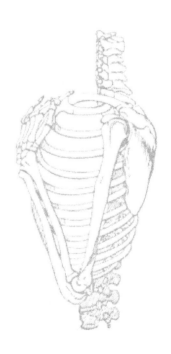

Reduce your speech, and
Shorten your hopes

You do not know the value
Of what you have until you
Lose it

The misery
Will not
Last forever

Strength
Does not lie in carrying heavy loads
Camels can do that
Strength
Lies in controlling your anger

Do not surround yourself with those
Who love this world
For if you become needy
They will leave you, and
If you become wealthy
They will envy you

My Lord
You know me better than I know myself

Learn your religion
Do not inherit it

It is easier to turn
A mountain into dust
Than to create love
In a heart that is filled
With hatred

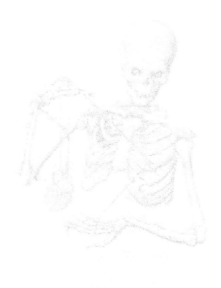

Do not use
The sharpness of the tongue
On the mother
Who taught you how
To speak

I am surprised at the man
Who searches for his lost item
While he has lost his own soul
And does not search for it

The biggest shame
Is to mock at something
That you have in
Yourself

There is a peace in
Solitude
Away from the evils of
People

Honour your guest
Even if he is not worthy
Of being honoured

Be soft
Without being weak
Be strong
Without being violent

A fool's mind
Is at the mercy
Of his tongue, and
A wise man's tongue
Is under the control
Of his mind

Do good
But never speak of it

The hypocrite
Sees fault in
Everyone except
In himself

A body will not become weak
Where the intention is strong

One
Who talks too much
Makes the most
Mistakes

Dislike
In yourself what you
Dislike
In others

Prefer to be the one who
Is defeated
While being just
Rather than the one
Who triumphs
While being unjust

The world
Is like a snake
Soft to touch
But full of venom

You will begin to heal
When you let go of past hurts
And forgive those
Who have wronged you

Refresh your minds
From time to time
For a tired mind
Becomes blind

Surely this world has turned its back
Announcing its departure
While
The hereafter has approached
Announcing its arrival

Two things define you;
Your patience when you
Have nothing
Your attitude when you
Have everything

Real death
Is to live in subjugation
Real life
Is dying as subjugators

What's yours
Will find you

Treat the members
Of your family
With love and respect
Because they act as wings
With which you

Fly

He who angers you
Controls you

Silence
That covers you with
Honour
Is better than speech that earns you
Regret

Do not talk about what you
Do not know
For what you know
Might be very little

Do not say
All that you
Know

Every deed is judged by the
Intention

Learn to be quiet
Just as you learn to talk
Because
If talking guides you
Silence protects you

If a man loves a thing
He becomes blind to its defects
His mind is predisposed to its favour
His sight and hearing lose the power
Of seeing and hearing realities
He cannot tolerate to see or hear
Anything
Against the object of his devotion

One who fears death cannot escape it
One who fears eternal life cannot secure it

Let go
Of what has passed

The richest of the rich
Is one who is not a prisoner to
Greed

Do not allow yourself to feel sorrow
For what is lost
Such as that it preoccupies you
From what is to come

The truest thing
Is Death

Lightning Source UK Ltd.
Milton Keynes UK
UKHW012234260221
379474UK00008B/469/J